Quotes!

MIRIAM SICILIANO

Quotes!
Copyright © 2021 by Miriam Siciliano

All rights reserved. No part of this publication may be reproduced, distributed, or transmitted in any form or by any means, including photocopying, recording, or other electronic or mechanical methods, without the prior written permission of the author, except in the case of brief quotations embodied in critical reviews and certain other non-commercial uses permitted by copyright law.

Tellwell Talent
www.tellwell.ca

ISBN
978-0-2288-6243-7 (Paperback)

*This book was created not by me but by the many
friends and family members who continuously
send me morning greetings with words of wisdom,
spiritual blessing and inspiring messages.
As I read through these messages time and time again, a
message in the form of a whisper was given to me to print
to share with the world. So, I have created this book.
I share these quotes with you with the hope that
you find them as enjoyable and informative
as me. I hope that in some way these messages
touch your core as they have touched mine.*

CHAPTER 1
Empowering Messages

Life is what we make it.
Always has been, always
Will be. Make today
Ridiculously amazing.

Let there be silence in your
Mind, warmth in your heart and
Peace in your soul.

May you find moments to
Make you smile.

Stay positive: say yes
To happiness and no
To stress.

Start your day with a smile
And positive thoughts.

May the gift of love,
The gift of peace,
The gift of hope,
The gift of happiness
And the gift of blessings
Be yours today and always.

Happiness can't be far
Behind a grateful heart
And a peaceful mind.

Inhale new and vital.
Exhale old and useless.

Stay positive and never give up.

When love resides in your heart
Life will always be beautiful

Every day is a miracle, so live
It with grace.
May your days be filled with fabulous
Thoughts, people and moments.

Every smile
Every loving word
Every kind action
Is a reflection of the
Beauty in our hearts.

Give the ones you love
The wings to fly
Roots to come back
And a reason to stay.

Never stop dreaming.

Don't be so focused on struggles
That you miss the
Gifts of today.

Patience and silence
Are two powerful energies.
Patience makes you
Mentally strong.
Silence makes you
Emotionally strong.

Life is a collection
Of moments.

Speak from your soul
And your heart will
Understand.

Some people are so special
That once they enter your life
It becomes richer.

Never forget the three
Power resources that
Are always available to you:
Love, Prayer and Forgiveness.

The first ever cordless phone
Was created by GOD.
He named it
Prayer.

Rejoice in hope.
Be patient in tribulation.
And
Be constant in prayer.

As children of God we can find
Joy in every day not because
It's always good but
Because GOD is.

When GOD decides to bless you
He will always cause situations
To come together in your
Favour no matter what others try to do.
No one can bless your blessing.

A smile is a spiritual perfume
You spray on and everyone
Benefits.

Today, let's remember that
Life gives no guarantees. It's
Uncertain and unpredictable.
Hence, it's our duty to make the
Most of it.

Until you spread your wings,
You will have no idea how
Far you can fly.
Life is not about finding yourself;
Life is about creating yourself.

Optimism is a happiness magnet.
Stay positive and good things and
Good people will be drawn to you.

Life is all about moving on
Accepting changes and
Looking forward to what makes you
Stronger and more complete.

I never think I have nothing.
I never think I have everything.
But I think I have something
And I can achieve anything.

When you arise in the morning,
Think of what a precious
Privilege it is to be alive.

May your day be blessed with all
Things bright and beautiful.

Life is full of possibilities.
Believe in yourself and
All that you are, and know
That there is something inside
You that is greater than any
Obstacle.

There are only two days
In the year that nothing
Can be done.
One is called yesterday and the other
Is called tomorrow.
Today is the only day to
believe, love and live.

Life is a collection of moments:
Some happy, some sad and
Some unforgettable.

Every day starts with some
Expectation, and every day ends
With some experience.

Don't think that time will
Change our lives.
Time only changes the opportunity.

Family is a little bit crazy:
A little bit loud but most
Of all
A whole lot of love.

A family does not have
To be perfect.
It just must unite.

Family is where life beings
And love never ends.

When we have each other,
We have everything.

Joy is never tomorrow.
It's always today.

Family is like music:
Some light notes
Some low notes
But always a beautiful song.

Always smile at life.
It will smile back
At you.

No problem can be solved
With tears and tension.

Lots of challenges can
Be met with a
Smile on your face
And positivity in
Your attitude.

Money is small coins.
Health is big coins.
Love is a lucky coin.
Friendship is a sweet coin.
And relationship is a gold coin.
Keep it safe.

No matter how good or bad
You think you have it,
Wake up every morning and
Be grateful for your life.

Having a sharp memory is
A quality of the brain.
But the ability to forget the
Unwanted things is a
Far better quality of life.
A friend is someone who
Listens to your crap,
Tells you it's crap
And listens some more.

If speaking kindly to plants
Can help them to grow,
Imagine what speaking kindly
To humans can do.

We fall, we break, we fail
But then
We rise, we heal, we overcome.

I am not this hair.
I am not this skin.
I am the soul that
Lives within.

When you arise in the morning,
Think of what a precious
Privilege it is to be
Alive to think, to breathe,
To love.

Between a million yesterdays
And a million tomorrows,
There is only one
Today.

Be selective with your battles.
Sometimes peace is better than
Being right.

Every end can be
A new beginning.

Morning is the best time
To remember all your
Favourite people who make
You happy so that you
Wake up with a smile.

New day
New life
New hope.

Be positive, and good
Things will happen.

Every day is a blessing
When you appreciate Life.

Relationships are insurance
Policies against loneliness.
They need to be renewed with
Regular premium of
Communication, feelings
And love.

We are like pencils:
The best part is inside.
We make marks as we touch
other lives.

The measure of happiness
And peace of mind is in
Our hearts.

The most wonderful place
To be is in someone's
Thoughts, prayers and heart.
Happiness is only when you
Can share it.

Always find time for
The things that make you
Feel happy to be alive.

The song of life has a
Beautiful rhythm. At
Times we forget the lyrics,
But if good people
Provide the melody then
Life's music plays on.

The most expensive thing
In the world is
TRUST:
It can talk years to earn
But only seconds to lose.

A smile speaks every language.

Every moment has love in it.
Every hour has happiness.
If you lose it, it becomes
A memory, and if you live it,
It becomes life.

All things are possible if
You have faith. Believe in
You and your abilities
With boundless vision and
Determination, motivation and
Dedication. Anything is
Achievable.

The game of life is like
A football:
You must tackle your problems,
Block your fears
And score your point when
You get the opportunity.

The power of one:
One step can start a journey,
One song can change a moment,
One smile can start a friendship,
One hug can lift a soul,
One candle can wipe out darkness,
One life can make a difference,
One word can start a prayer,
One hope can life a spirit
And one touch can show you care.

Give but don't allow yourself
to be used.
Love but don't allow your heart to
be abused.
Trust but don't be naïve.
Listen but don't lose your voice.

Listen to your heart:
It may be on your left but it's
Always right.

Live your life and forget your age.
What matters most is how
You see yourself.
Today, choose to dance to
The rhythm of heart.

Shine bright, share your light
And let your spirit soar.

Respect is the most important element
Of your personality.
It's like an investment:
It will be returned to you with
Profit.

Always wear a smile
Because your smile is a
Reason for many others
To smile.

Beauty never gets lost as we get older.
It moves from your face to
Your heart.

Life is full of give and take.
Give thanks and take
Nothing for granted.

May every sunrise
Hold more promise.
May every sunset
Hold more peace.

The best exercise is walking.
Walk away from thoughts that
Steal your happiness.

Life, family and friends are
Worth more than all the
Money in the world.

Be positive: good things will happen.

Many relationships cannot be
Evaluated in terms of money
Or gains.
Some investments
Never make a profit
But they still make you reach.

History will remember this war:
A war fought by doctors and not soldiers,
A war fought by soap and not guns,
A war fought by keeping distance
not contact,
A war fought at home and not on the
Battlefield.

Never give up.
Never lose hope.
Always have faith because
It allows you to cope.

Every day stars with some expectations
And every day ends with experience.
This is called life,
So, enjoy the day every day.
Sometimes you just must die
A little inside in order to be
Reborn and rise again
To be a stronger and wiser
Version of yourself.

The moment you accept
Responsibility for everything
In your life is the moment you
Gain the power to change
Anything in your life.

Everything happens for a reason.
That reason causes change.
Sometimes it hurts,
Sometimes it's hard,
But in the end, it's all for the best.

CHAPTER 2

Spiritual Messages

Life is a miracle, and every breath we
Take is a gift from God.

May your day be peaceful and joyful
And may God continue to guide your path.

May God walk with you today and
In the days ahead.

Where does my help come from?
It comes from GOD.

May your day be blessed with all
Things bright and beautiful.

Be grateful for each day. Let your
Gratitude be your attitude
Because each day you live is
A gift from God.

No matter how smooth or
How rough this day is, God
Is with you each and
Every step of the way.

May your day begin with a smile on
Your face, love in your heart
And happiness for your soul
To embrace.

Life is better when you cry a little
Laugh a little
And be thankful for everything
You've got.

A great thinker was asked
What is the meaning of life?
He replied that life itself has no meaning.
Life is an opportunity to create meaning.

May you enjoy the blessings
and favour of God today.
Enjoy the beauty that the
day brings.

The love of a family life
Is the greatest blessing.

Life is peaceful when
You rest on God's word.

Be a channel of joy.
Be a blessing to others.

Prayer is the only gift
We can give to the people
We care for, so on the
Wings of love I pray
To God to take care and
Bless you every day of your life.

My life is blessed with
The most amazing people.
Thank you for being part
Of my life.

Be happy with what you have.
Keep working on what
You love and remember.
A happy lift begins by
Saying
Thank you, Lord.

Smile: life is short so
Enjoy it while you can.

Only you oversee your happiness.

May your day start great
And just keep getting
Better.

The only person you should
Try and beat is the
Person you were
Yesterday.

Take the time to enjoy
The wonder and the beauty
Of each moment.

A smile can open a heart
Faster than a key
Can open a door.
So, keep smiling.

Use your eyes to see
The possibilities, not
The problem.

It doesn't matter how long
We live,
How we live is what matters.

In life we cannot always
Do great things,
But we can do small things
With great love.

Each moment in a day
Has its own value:
Morning brings hope,
Afternoon brings faith,
Evenings brings love,
Night brings rest.
I wish you find them all for you.

Count your life by smiles,
Not tears.
Count your age by friends,
Not years.

Happiness comes when
You believe in what you are doing,
Know what you are doing
And love what you are doing.

Life doesn't allow for us
To go back and fix what we
Have done wrong in the past,
But it does allow for us
To live each day better
Than the last one.

Accept both compliment and
Criticism because it takes both
Sun and rain for a flower
To grow.

May your day be filled
With fabulous thoughts,
Fabulous people and
Fabulous moments.

Take a chance,
Follow your heart and
Be happy.

Do small things with
Great love.

Think good thoughts,
Say good words and
Do good deeds all the time.
WE are not called to be
Victorious.
We are called to be wise,
Strong and kind.

Live the life you want.

We all have the power to heal.

What I know for sure
Is that transformation happens
When you dare to be awakened
To greater heights.

Appreciate where you are in your journey
Even if it's not where you want to be.
Every season serves a purpose.

Happiness keeps you sweet,
Trials keeps you strong,
Sorrow keeps you human,
Failure keeps you humble
And
Courage keeps you going.

Good morning is not just a
Greeting, it signifies a hope
That this beautiful morning
Brings a smile to your face
And happiness in your life.

When love resides in your
Heart, life is always beautiful.

Behind you, all your memories,
Before you, all your dreams,
Around you, all who love you,
Within you, all you need.

The happiness of your life
Depends on the quality of your
Thoughts.

Believe in your heart that
Something wonderful is
Going to happen to you.

A smile makes you attractive.
It changes your mood,
It relieves stress and it
Helps you to stay positive.

Smile because it's good for your heart.
Laugh because it's good for your soul.
Love because it keeps you living.

Bless everyone because
It's blessed to be a blessing.

Between yesterday's mistake
And tomorrow's hope,
There is a fantastic opportunity called today:
Live it, Love it,
Make this day yours.

Life is better when you
Cry a little,
Laugh a lot and be
Thankful for all you have.

May joy find you, may love surround you,
May laughter sing with you
And may God walk with you always.

Pray when you feel like worrying.
Give thanks when you feel like complaining.
Keep going when you feel like quitting.

As you get older you will understand
It's not about your looks,
It's about the person you become.

Friends are flowers in the
Garden of life.

Plant your garden with the things
You want to see grow:
LOVE,
HOPE,
COURAGE,
FAITH.

The best and most beautiful things in life
Cannot be seen or touched.
They can only be felt
By the heart.
Speak from your soul, and
Your heart will understand.

To everything there is a season,
A time for every purpose
Under the sun.

Be thankful and cherish
Everything that you have.
You never know how long
You will have it.

A beautiful life does not
Just happen.
It is built day by day through
Prayer, humility, sacrifice
And love.

Strength doesn't come from what
You can do.
Strength comes from overcoming
The things you thought you couldn't.
The biggest difference between
Money and time is that
You always know how much money you have
But you never know much time you have.
Enjoy every moment of your life.

Do not let others pull you
Into their storm.
Pull them into your peace.

Life is a miracle and every breath we
Take is a gift.

A good deed is never lost.
He who sows courtesy reaps
Friendship
And those who plant kindness
Gather love.

Monday is the beginning
Of a wonderful week:
Live it.
Life becomes more meaningful
When you realize that you
Will never get the same moment
Twice.

Start your day with a smile,
Calmness of mind,
Coolness of emotions
And a heart filled
With gratitude.

Never miss an opportunity to
Put a smile on someone's face:
It may be the only one they
Get today.

The sweetest moments in life
Come not with the greeting
You received, but with the
Thought that someone wishes
The best for you every day

Life isn't meant to be easy,
It's meant to be lived.

Life is about enjoying
Where you are, enjoying who you are
And consistently improving
Both.

Let there be silence in
Your mind,
Warmth in your heart
And peace in your soul

Sometimes what looks like
An obstacle in your path
Is a gift meant to move
You in another direction.

Another day is another blessing
Of life.

Take nothing for granted and
Think of every breath as a gift.

May the blessings of this day
Radiate through your smile.

As you wake up this day,
Say a silent prayer of thanks
For yet another new day.

I pray that the love of Jesus
Surrounds you and gives you peace.

Let every day be a chance:
A chance to be a better person,
A chance to enjoy life,
A chance to correct mistakes,
A chance to forgive,
A chance to love.
Don't miss your chance from
God as you wake up this day.

Pray not because you need something
But because you
Have a lot to be thankful for.

There is nothing ahead of you that is
Bigger or stronger than the
Power of God.

As long as you have God,
You have hope.

Don't neglect to do what
Is good and share, as God
Is always pleased with your
Sacrifices.

When God has selected you
It doesn't matter who
Rejects you because
God's favour outweighs
All opposition.

May you know that God is
By your side, and may
You feel His tender love
With you every moment
Of the day.

Today is going to be a great
Day. Trust in God and
Have faith.

A man's heart plans his way,
But the Lord directs the steps.
Whoever trusts in the Lord,
Happy is he.

Be of good courage and He
Shall strengthen your heart.
Have hope in the
Lord.

You are the creator of your garden.
Plant kindness and compassion.
Water with love and
Gratitude all the days of
Your life.

One of the joys in life is
Waking up each day with
Thoughts that somewhere
Someone cares enough
To send a warm greeting.

The most useful asset of a person
Is not a head full of knowledge
But a heart full of love,
Ears open to listen and
Hands willing to help.

All tomorrows depend
On today.

Today let us remember
That life gives no guarantees.
Life is uncertain and unpredictable.
Hence, it's our duty to make
The most of it.

It's Sunday, therefore
I am 100% motivated to do nothing.

A river never reverses,
So live life like a river. Forget
The past and focus on the
Future.

As you grow older,
It's less important to have
More friends and more important
To have real friends.
Happiness is not measured
By the amount of money you
have, it's measured by the
wonderful people in your life.

Soft attitudes always create
Strong relationships.

Patience is when you are
Supposed to be mad
But you choose to understand.

A beautiful heart
Is better than a
Thousand beautiful faces.

Hope is the power that gives
A person the confidence to
Step out and try.

The more balanced
You are with yourself,
The more difficult it is for others
To disturb you.

Be happy, smile,
Be fearless and most
Importantly be you.

www.ingramcontent.com/pod-product-compliance
Lightning Source LLC
LaVergne TN
LVHW091935070526
838200LV00068B/1247